Hatcher Family Myth

Deserter or Hero? Search for the Truth

by

Rev. Jerry Heydenberk

DORRANCE
PUBLISHING CO
EST. 1920
PITTSBURGH, PENNSYLVANIA 15238

The contents of this work, including, but not limited to, the accuracy of events, people, and places depicted; opinions expressed; permission to use previously published materials included; and any advice given or actions advocated are solely the responsibility of the author, who assumes all liability for said work and indemnifies the publisher against any claims stemming from publication of the work.

All Rights Reserved
Copyright © 2020 by Rev. Jerry Heydenberk

No part of this book may be reproduced or transmitted, downloaded, distributed, reverse engineered, or stored in or introduced into any information storage and retrieval system, in any form or by any means, including photocopying and recording, whether electronic or mechanical, now known or hereinafter invented without permission in writing from the publisher.

Dorrance Publishing Co
585 Alpha Drive
Pittsburgh, PA 15238
Visit our website at *www.dorrancebookstore.com*

ISBN: 978-1-6442-6197-2
eISBN: 978-1-6442-6333-4

Dedicated to
Marty Russell
gatherer and transmitter
of timely family history
and
William Carl Heydenberk
my great-grandfather whose story
I am proud to restore here

Chicago, vibrant city of industrial growth and swagger in 1800s America.

Big Chicago in Civil War Days

Chicago. The very name conjures up extravagant growth, vitality and raging economy in 1860s America.

A young, impressionable Carl William Hatcher had looked forward to his trip to the big city for weeks. His intention was to attend the big livestock convention to gain new breeder's information. He also hoped to engage in making new contacts in his breeder's field.

Visiting the big city of busyness, growth and swagger would be an awesome adventure for this country boy. He meant to make the most of visiting the city whose reputation as a world leader was just beginning to develop.

Chicago at the outbreak of the Civil War was a hotbed politically, economically and socially. Its assets counted dozens of mills, slaughterhouses and lumberyards. It had become the railroad capital of

America, its hub the largest in the railroad industry. The burgeoning "windy city" was home to 500 factories. People shopping downtown could have the best of European styles as the world's fashions and literary treasures were on view in the city facing Lake Michigan. Its marvelous water routes brought many goods and purchases to Chicago.

Chicago boasted the greatest primary grain port, hosted the largest lumber market of the world and was a growing cultural center sponsoring shows and art events that drew patrons from around the world. Founded in 1837, Chicago was the world's fastest growing city for several decades. Its population soared from 16,000 to 109,000 in just 13 years.

Illinois was the state of Abraham Lincoln, who became US President in 1861. While the state stayed in the Union during the Civil War (1861-65), seven states, beginning with South Carolina in 1860, seceded from the Union. This left the great experiment of the United States of America tattered and in disarray as President Lincoln entered office.

It was this Chicago that drew Carl in his desire to appreciate firsthand the offerings of Chi-Town. His interest in exploring more of the national swine breeding field would grow his business contacts. He was anxious to know more about the big city.

Carl hailed from DeKalb, Illinois, just 40 miles west of Chicago. He had studied livestock breeding records with increased interest prior to the livestock convention. He was serious about his vocation and wanted to enlarge his capability in the field. Selfishly, he even considered finding a qualified "female companion". Unmarried women in Aurora were scarce. At 21 Carl believed he needed to find a suitable mate because he was ready for marriage. He hoped to find a woman he could introduce to his farm operation. Could he possibly convince her to share with him in that operation? High hopes indeed for a young bachelor from the country.

The Galena & Chicago Union Railroad gave Carl and fellow passengers access from the rural areas to DeKalb to downtown Chicago.

Riding off to the city in pleasure, Carl lavished the plush passenger car. Its bold interior was decorated with red crimson cushions, gaslights and offered an array of menu delicacies. This amounted to a novel experience for Carl. "What a luxury this would be to have this train car parked near the barn where I live," he remarked to a fellow passenger. "It would be like having heaven in my back yard." Carl at best was a man of hyperbole.

Carl holds theatre program as he chats with Malinda Mason.

Carl Meets Southern Belle at Theatre

Livestock conventions offer a variety of presentations by experts including care of range-feeding cattle, proper saddles for herding ponies and keeping water tanks warm during the winter season. Carl soon tired of so much information, so one evening he and new friend, Michael Jacob, also from Illinois, decided to explore the city's entertainment offerings. Reading the *Chicago Daily Journal*, Carl noted an original Vaudeville act that was playing at the downtown theatre. Michael, who also bought a ticket, had a conflict so he gave his to Carl to use as he chose. Undeterred, Carl dressed in a warm tweed jacket and donned a bowtie for the dress-up occasion. As he entered the theatre and proceeded to his seat, Carl lost hold of his program. Reaching across the aisle seat to reclaim the dropped paper, he roughly bumped a lady walking by with his shoulder.

"Truly, I beg your pardon, Miss," Carl exclaimed in his most polite manner. "I was only trying to pursue a pesky program that dropped from my clasp. I hope you will excuse me."

Her response was equally as charming, "I understand completely. These programs can be so troublesome, falling just as you think you have an honest hold of them."

"What I mean to say," Carl responded quickly, "is that the impulsive action of my shoulder should not have been in so offensive a space. At least let me know your name that I may apologize more properly."

"Why my name, as you so sweetly inquire, is Malinda Lee," she answered with a hint of flirtation in her southern dialect. "How nice of you to be so noble as to charge your unruly shoulder with the unmeant harm."

"May I inquire of you then, Malinda Lee, if you would occupy the seat next to me? My name is Carl and the man who was to sit here was called away to another place."

"I accept," her cheeks flushed as she accepted, "but please let me go to my seating companions and inform my younger sister and her girlfriend that I will be sitting elsewhere." Malinda did not say where she would be seated as her sister, Savannah, would no doubt tell their father and then she would be in trouble again. Accepting an invitation to sit with a total stranger in a darkened theatre was not something tolerated by her up-class parents. Oh well, she would just tell Savannah and her friend she was invited to join a former college instructor and her family. Oh gee, a little lie, but she could reason it was only a little one. One her parents would accept.

With that thought in mind and a quick swish of her skirt the young woman went to inform her companions. This left Carl to recount his good fortune. First, it was his delightful opportunity to meet such a refined woman who chose to attend the theatre when he did. Second, his friend had left his seat ticket for Carl to use for just this occasion. He could now gladly offer the ticket to the coquettish south-ern belle, Malinda Lee. He was glad he did because their conversation was instantly engaging. Humor and just plain happy talk were items of the evening.

In the brief time following the final curtain, Carl learned the de-lightful 19-year-old was a woman he was determined to know better. How fortunate that the young man met a woman equal to his hope for future female companionship.

Carl and Malinda Pose for Photographer

Carl and Malinda Described

Malinda convinced Carl to have their photographs taken by a professional in Chicago. He agreed, and the picture of the couple's early courtship days is recorded in this attractive pose.

Malinda was attractively attired in a green, frilly dress with a matching silk scarf and clutch purse. Standing 5'5", Malinda wore her frilly dress and gold shoes with a southern kind of dignity. Her shoe color complemented her bright auburn hair and red-violet lipstick. Her only facial flaw was a slight down-turn of her mouth, which gave her a pouty look. Nevertheless, what an elegant show of 19th century fashion she made.

Carl was ruggedly handsome himself; he considered himself a catch for any woman. His deeply tanned skin displayed the outdoor work he enjoyed. When on the job, you could find him in weathered jeans and heavy farm boots. His dark-brown, curly hair showed what a real farmer looked like. A 5'9" lithe frame allowed him to easily face all the work needed for raising, lifting and sorting over 100 pigs each farrowing season. Strength, coordination and a good deal of patience was needed to handle pigs from 20 to over 200 pounds of vibrating, lively flesh.

An only son, Carl lost a younger sister who drowned in a farm pond at age 5. Carl was 21 and naturally grieved the death. He was unable to enjoy any adult consolation made available to him. Tragically, both his parents died in a freak horse carriage mishap. A deer sprinting across the road had frightened the skittish horse. The horse jumped into a small canyon pulling the carriage behind it. John and Helen Hatcher rode the precarious vehicle until it turned over. Neither parent walked away. The horse broke loose from the toppled carriage and disappeared into the undergrowth.

Still he had a kind of shield against outside influence; his manliness had an obvious flaw: he had suffered greatly and had no answer for grief. This had an effect on his emotional growth and the manner of developing new relationships.

Planning almost as if he knew the future, Carl's father left his son with a broad background for operating the swine operation. Training him from herd management to active record keeping was part of the son's training. Meanwhile, Carl's mother taught him to cook and to learn the tasks of housekeeping. In fact, the young man was prepared to seek a life partner after the family deaths. He was lonely on the mid-sized farm and yearned for a companion to share his love for the farm. Yet somehow the young man maintained his humor and light-heartedness that edged out the grief of his life.

Rescuing him from this aloneness was the affirming parenting his father's brother, Raymond and his wife Cecelia Hatcher, offered. Carl lived in their home a full two years while riding his horse to the swine farm for watering and feeding chores. He only returned to the silent farmhouse after recovering from mourning the loss of three family lives. Thus, he was only coming off the grief period and ready to find someone new in his life when he met the lovely Malinda.

Presently, Carl was with Malinda at the theatre. After the Vaudeville acts that featured a juggler and seven acrobats plus a blustery clown, which he and Malinda Lee enjoyed with shared laughter, Carl walked his date back to her parent's home. They had plenty of time for light talk over the nine blocks in unseasonably warm weather. Carl told Malinda the good things about farm life, speaking with insight and enthusiasm. He omitted the smelly waste of active barnyards to leave a more positive influence on his listener. Solemnly, he spoke of the loss of sister and parents. Then he switched to the subject closest to his heart: the joys and benefits of raising pigs.

"You cannot believe how soft and cuddly the baby piglets can be," Carl exclaimed. Seeing them several days after birth, was the time he referred to. That was the time to hold their warm bodies with a fuzzy down of hair and delightful smell. A sow's healthy delivery and feel of the snuggly piglets made him affirm the reason he had chosen the farm life.

"Do they ever bite you or do they feed on someone else?" Malinda asked innocently.

"They don't bite me, but as they grow they require feeding. The mother sow takes care of that. I just clean the farrowing stalls and try to keep up with the sows about to give birth."

Carl then explained how he had to occasionally scour open fields to follow his wandering sows post-delivery. "They keep me on my toes trying to figure ahead where they are going to have their babies. They seem to prefer natural field nests to the prepared farrowing stalls I have for them."

"Oh," Malinda rejoined, trying to picture what on earth he was talking about. She marveled at the low birthing pens for the mother sows only 3½ to 4 feet tall. Also catching her attention was how Carl put wood railings along the side to protect the piglets when the sows lay down to expose their under belly and teats for feeding.

Other aspects of the 220-acre farm included a fenced pig pen, an outer shed for the milking cow and a stall in the barn now full of straw bales for cow and his horse, King. Farming equipment for planting and harvesting grain crops to feed the swine herd Carl kept at Uncle Raymond's farm just up the gravel road.

Carl did swine management that included sorting barrows from guilts and new mother sows and their offspring. Preventing sows that had just delivered litters from laying on their piglets was a real danger. Farm publications advised that every litter of seven or more newborn pigs would show a good return on investment; having fewer than seven survive represented a loss. Lost income resulted from overrun in terms of feed, vaccination and confinement costs.

After walking Malinda to the door, Carl turned to bid her good night. But Malinda urged, "Carl, please come in to meet my parents. Dad and Mom would be happy to meet the man who walked me this long way home," she coaxed.

Upon entering the door, Carl's eyes took in the large entry room with winding staircase and upper loft of doors, presumably for bedrooms. Or maybe they were rooms more like "the library" that Malinda ushered him into with rows of walled bookcases and some comfortable easy chairs.

Thomas and Deedee Mason's home was decidedly on the rich side of Chicago, in the Glendale subdivision. They had no sons but a younger daughter, Savannah. The family moved from Nashville, Tennessee three months ago to the big city. The portly Thomas had relocated his family to Chicago to begin new employment as a master iron worker.

The Masons welcomed Carl with thanks for walking their daughter home; nevertheless, he felt he did not measure up with his farm background. He did make a favorable impression on the younger sister who seemed taken with his midwestern twang, but not so the parents. After he left, Thomas and Deedee wondered out loud why Malinda had picked a farm boy for her first date in Chicago.

Mother: "Don't you think bringing a farm hand home was a bit audacious?"

Father: "What kind of income does the young man manage from his, what did you say, a pig farm in the country? Does he make as much wage as a daily iron and steel maker?"

Malinda: "Mama, papa, I just had a chance meeting with the handsome young man at the theatre. What more can you expect of this polite, funny fellow that I bring home to offer some hospitality. You both need to be more accepting of my new friends, especially one who walks me home such a distance."

To their daughter's happy exclamations, father and mother could offer no reply.

Afterward, since Carl was only to be in Chicago four days, Malinda suggested a real first date for the next day. They found a local Italian restaurant, their happy conversation establishing a warm bond. Talking late into that evening, they shared personal likes and aspirations. When Carl returned home, he and Melinda exchanged letters and a couple more visits. Hence, the six months of their companionship passed rapidly, and they sensed their courtship was heading in a good direction.

Carl seeks permission to ask Malinda's father for her hand.

Carl Asks for Malinda's Hand

Believing their connection was progressing positively, at least as far as they could see, the young couple began to discuss the prospect of marriage. When Carl worked up courage to approach Malinda Lee's father, he found serious Thomas Mason more than a little troubled about the details of joining these two lives. Thomas found the relationship of a union between a "country farm boy" and his exceptional daughter difficult to accept. He liked even less that Malinda at 19 would move away and live with a man who was just 21 on a country farm.

As with most fathers, he wanted Malinda Lee to be well cared for and given the style of life to which she was accustomed. Thomas had moved his wife and their two daughters from Nashville to assume employment as an experienced iron worker. Chicago was in the rapidly growing iron industry of pre-Civil War days. During the time thousands working in large iron and steel mills labored to turn iron ore into steel and shape steel into a variety of products. Chicago became home to six iron foundries, benefiting from its excellent location on Lake Michigan and easy access to river transportation. Mr. Mason introduced his shrewd businessman's mind and capabilities into this booming industry as a professional steelmaker. He gained a top supervisor's position due to knowledge learned in previous experience in Nashville.

Carl had anticipated that Thomas would take a hard look at his farm operation and income for the past year. Mr. Mason's business position offered a solid work record for comparison. So, Carl set about to build a solid case of good swine purchases and farrowing records that led to substantial sales at the great Chicago stockyards. He also gathered his best, most convincing character as a certified swine breeder to show the older gentleman how his daughter would be welcomed to the regular routine of a farm life.

"Your daughter has already learned the joy of holding warm, cuddly piglets. She will enjoy watching them grow. And Malinda's interest will grow as she takes in the healthy farm life and enjoys watching the sunrise and sunset as if it were in her own living room."

"Yes, but can my college-age and flighty daughter accustom herself to regular farm life with all of its inconveniences?" Thomas queried. "You see, she can be very demanding in her likes and dislikes. Besides, her college education makes her more selective of the kind of lifestyle she chooses."

"Not to worry, sir," Carl responded. "We have already cleared that hurdle of what she will come to love on the farm. Malinda has proved equal to tasks from her previous visits to the farm. I can and will provide for your daughter's expenses and fashion needs."

A reluctant Thomas listened to Carl's discourse patiently. Eventually his objections to the marriage were worn down by the young man's persistence. Carl's promise to treat Malinda with all due respect sealed the deal.

"Yes, I believe your intentions for giving our daughter a good life are sincere. Her mother and I accept your request for Malinda Lee's hand in marriage. Just be sure you give our Malinda the kind of life she deserves. Or I assure you, your name will not be remembered long in our family," the stern Thomas affirmed.

With a wedding set for June, the Masons arranged for an impressive ceremony and rented a banquet hall in downtown Chicago. A college friend was maid of honor. Malinda's younger sister, Savannah, was bridesmaid. Carl's new friend, Michael, served as best man. Oh, what a delightful time to experience the huge hall and to dance in the semi-private side room until the nighttime stars appeared.

Tastefully set in the middle of a fancy rented hall, the wedding site was the formal and happy scene where the Masons presented their elder daughter into the Chicago society. Carl, despite being amazed at all the falderol of newspaper coverage, was seemingly in the way as so many photographers were present to take pictures of the coming-out Mason daughter.

Perhaps Thomas Mason was hoping a new suitor would come forward since he still had doubts Carl could hold his own against a true man of Chicago society. So began the presentation of Malinda Mason in fashion and in handsome wedding attire.

Becoming a debutante plus the wedding celebration, was like a dream for the sparkling Malinda. Introducing a deb in "polite society" marks the formal presentation of a young lady and introduces her as a mature adult. The young lady loved the attention. Was this something Carl needed to be aware of? Was it noteworthy to carry concern for her actions in this spectacular event arranged for the Masons for her benefit?

The couple honeymooned at Whihala Beach, a scenic honeymoon spot off Chicago's south skyline facing onto Lake Michigan. The popular honeymoon location was also secured thanks to the Mason family's generosity. "What a wonderful gift," Carl mused. He was finally able to take five days away from farm life and now lounged comfortably in a deck chair on the sandy beach of Whihala. "Your parents are so gracious in hosting our wedding and paying for this honeymoon spot. What a wonderful place to relax!" he concluded.

"Oh I agree," considered the new bride. "With your uncle caring for the farm, you, dear husband, can relax and enjoy the beach and lovely boating activities provided for us. Come, let's go and see about renting a sailboat for sailing up the inlet just off the lake."

So went the days following the wedding as the young couple enjoyed each other's tenderness and learned what it meant to be a happily married husband and wife.

Initial days on the farm were just as romantic. Malinda learned how to cook under Carl's patient instruction. Carl learned what it was to share household duties. He already relished the companionship of a woman equal to his desires. They made love in the bedroom the wife had decorated tastefully, and in the proper time they welcomed their first child, Jonathan. Malinda's mother, Deedee came to assist after the birth-assisted delivery by a local midwife.

Trouble loomed on the horizon, however. Malinda began to grow more isolated with farm life, missing the social life available in the city. She also missed the advantages of a hospital. Before a second son, Willis, was born, she told her husband she would no longer have patience to birth this child by a midwife. She steadfastly demanded delivery at a Chicago hospital with a medical doctor attending.

Try as he might, Carl found he just could not dissuade his stubborn wife. He chalked her fancy needs up to her family upbringing and two years of college that gained her a business certificate. Malinda said the college years enlarged her perspective on women's rights and the social things of life. Unhappily, Carl accepted his resolute wife's complaints as valid. He agreed she could deliver their second child at the Chicago Cook County Hospital. Such were the needs of a disgruntled wife: she demanded to be pleased, not humored because she was female.

With the two sons, John and then Willis, Malinda was now completely outside her comfort level. Mama Deedee Mason came to assist in child-raising and stayed at the Hatcher home long enough to clearly see her daughter's decided dislike to farm life. Malinda was trying her best to adjust to a small farm home, but naturally missed the relationship she had with younger sister, Savannah, and her parent's social life.

"You should have anticipated this fact of differences," the mother chided. "You were so concerned with rushing into a marriage that mismatched two people of such different backgrounds and tastes. I only hope your sister will have more sense than you did. You should share with her your choices, so she will refrain from the same mistakes you made.

"Mama." Malinda responded with an edge to her voice, "I accept my mistakes, but Carl is a good husband. He is a caring father and is trying to make me like the farm. And he was sensitive enough to agree with me on the hospital and a doctor's delivery for our second child. Just give us a little longer," she reasoned, "to make our lives better."

Carl volunteers for duty in Union Army over wife's desires.

Carl Chooses Federal Cause Over Malinda

Carl Hatcher was a man of Federal Government persuasion. This should have forewarned his future wife of serious differences to consider in their future. Whether proslavery or antislavery? That was not a topic discussed lightly in their home. Carl thought he knew the southern sympathies of the Mason family, but he failed to realize how deeply these roots ran. Joining discussion on North versus South was too controversial with their regional differences—Carl from the Midwest and Malinda representing the stately South.

Had the couple spoken honestly and clearly on this subject before they wed, it might have eliminated many concerns. Were the issues of personal convictions concerning the war sufficiently explored? Was conversation ever joined about their differences over North unification and South secessionism? Was Carl negligent in taking the lead as the senior person in their discussions? Surely, such opposing views needed to be discussed for stability in the marriage. Concerns of this nature only seemed to grow as the terrible war progressed.

Civil War records showed some 26,000 Chicagoans were called to join the military and Carl wanted to volunteer with them from Illinois. Even so, thousands would lose their lives. This was not a consideration of Carl's. His desire was foremost to serve with the Union Army, support the U.S. Constitution and offer opposition to those advocating slavery on lofty and prosperous plantations. Very simple rationale. Easily defended. Subject closed.

Melinda's parents, the Masons, had long identified with the Confederacy, beginning their lives in the southern mindset. Although it required relocating from a comfortable home served by five slaves to a city in the north, Thomas believed it would benefit his family both financially and socially. In fact he had already joined a craftsman's guild; meanwhile, Deedee was a new member of several women's clubs.

Carl had no such concerns about introducing his family to Chicago society. He had other decisions that needed consideration. He had come to a decision that morning that would have lasting consequences for his family. The previous day he and Malinda had argued about his desire to volunteer for military service. He had his say, and this contributed to her response of anguish and temperamental opposition.

"Malinda, the North needs dedicated volunteers to fight for saving the Union," Carl stated. "Freeing indentured people is a cause I share with President Lincoln." He expounded how he firmly opposed a system that bound one person to work for another, denying individual freedom, regardless of color.

"Carl, you are not being fair. My parents owned five slaves who served our family back home. They always treated me quite well, thank you!"

"Malinda Lee, I see that my service in the Union Army would support the insensitive stand many people in the South have against the black race." This was not a good thing to say to his beleaguered wife. Her temper flared, and her tiny mouth drooped even lower in disgust.

"Well, I can see that you have no idea about slavery! It has been in the interest of southern families for years! You do not know what you are saying! Having slaves is an important part of culture in the South! A president like Jefferson Davis," she countered, "is trying to maintain that practice as shown by the states seceding against Mr. Lincoln's unfortunate policies."

Try as he might, Carl could not budge his wife from her rigid position. Having two-year's maturity over Malinda should have determined his leadership in the family, but he failed to take advantage of this responsibility. Where was his family leadership in this life-changing discussion with his wife?

Owning servants had been important for the Mason family in Tennessee. And she maintained her parents had treated their slaves well, providing a secure home for them. They had their places, Malinda countered, as cooks, maids and butlers. She had obediently come to rely on their services. Carl certainly did not know what growing up in a slave-owning family was like, she opined. She would not give her forced approval for opposing the idea of owning slaves by fighting in a war. He was fighting for the wrong cause, she reasoned, and that was that.

Malinda and son John on stairs wait anxiously for dad's return.

Malinda Decries Husband's Absence

"Mommy, where's Daddy? He's not home yet."

Speaking from the top step of the staircase, John was clad in pajamas as he looked down at his mother. Rubbing sleepy eyes, he stammered out, "D-daddy told me he would t-tuck me into bed t-tonight and h-he's not home. Did he f-forget, Mommy?"

As he spoke, the little boy placed his hand on the top rung of the staircase. The gleaming staircase shone with just the right mixture of stain and varnish. The finished wood was applied with the firmness and lightness of his father's hands. Such a man is cherished by his family, but now is late for supper and very late to meet a promise to his son.

It was unusual for Carl to pass up the chance to spend special time with his sons. He was a conscientious father who doted on John and Willie's attention. Where Malinda was strict, wanting the boys to show proper behavior around adults, Carl was more lenient. Malinda was quick to correct them for lapses in good behavior; Carl enjoyed the boys' antics and laughed along with them. John always took the lead and younger Willie followed in putting both into a real pickle. Like the time John put the toad in Mrs. Fogg's handbag, and Willie put a spoonful of salt into Mr. Hardy's tea.

John's explanation was particularly revealing as he stammered, "F-father, h-her bag had a frog p-picture on the top, so I d-dropped the toad in it so it wouldn't be l-lonesome."

Those were times of undeniable pleasure for father and sons. They were so inventive, Carl was quick to tell his adult friends. He also made it a point to inform victims of the boys' mischief to restore order before bedlam ensued. This was essential when company came for a visit and nodded approval over the cute little Hatcher boys.

Malinda, because she was sheltered as a girl and not used to being around children, had difficulty just enjoying John and Willis. They were not only unruly at times but sometimes just unmannerly. Manners were a big thing to her, and strict obedience was a necessity. The children must learn obedience and proper behavior at all times. She planned frequent trips to Chicago so her mother could help corral the boys. They definitely needed the grown-up female companion agreeable to their growth pattern, and mother Deedee provided that relationship.

Malinda was obviously beside herself when John's britches were stained from climbing a ripening mulberry tree. Willis meantime became fascinated with a rose bush and came home with lots of scratches on his face and hands from Mrs. Bloom's house. No bleeding however, much to Malinda's relief. She told Carl as soon as he walked in the front door, and he had difficulty restraining a chuckle from her explanation. She adamantly informed her husband of the purplish blobs on John's trouser shorts and Willie's scratched body. Then she watched for his expression to change, but Carl thought the boys' ingenuity in finding ways to amuse themselves quite amusing. Nevertheless, he was careful to maintain his solemn bearing in Malinda's presence.

Malinda glanced up at John whom she had put to bed hours earlier. She wore a simple cotton work dress and colorful, patterned apron. Attempting to find anything to keep her hands busy, she too, waited patiently for John's father to return as she labored in the kitchen. She had finished baking bread for the supper meal and was now attempting to clean up. How was she to answer an anxious son? She wondered again why Carl had not returned home as evening darkness settled over the town.

DeKalb was the only home she had known since leaving her parents in Chicago for marriage five years ago. It was growing to become the 18th largest city in Illinois and its rail head was growing as well. But it was not Chicago with its tall buildings and societal opportunities.

The Hatcher home was small and not hospitable for hosting women's groups from the church, a fact Malinda found disheartening. Now, about her husband. What if Carl had taken their last discussion so seriously. Had he decided to leave her for this unfinished argument with two small sons to raise by herself? Why would he want to do that? Why did she feel so ignored? John and Willis grew somber in their father's absence. Their sunny dispositions and playtime actvities grew methodical without Carl's joyful participation in the boys' antics. John expressed it peevishly, "If Dad were here, we'd have our best friend back. Mom would be nicer and Grandma Mason less strict."

During her husband's absence, she was feeling lonely although she knew she shouldn't. If only Carl's farm work didn't keep him away from home so long. And then there was the disagreeable conversation last evening that stemmed from his desire to join the army. Why did it have to be the Union Army? Her parents were supporters of the old, traditional South, and she knew full well they would not take kindly to his choice to side with the North.

"Why couldn't he find work closer to home?" Malina wondered thinking of her personal comfort needs. Her husband's 220-acres with 180 acres of wheat and corn, and the single milk cow, provided only a modest income. His efforts were in earnest, she knew. Still, why couldn't her hard-working husband take a job nearer the big city? Why not take the family back to her home? she mused. Why couldn't he just join one of the Confederate outfits?

"Daddy will be home soon, little one," she tried to sound reassuring but sensed she was failing. What would she tell her parents if Carl had indeed left to join the army? What would she tell her farm neighbors and people at church? She had made some friends in the local congregation, but most women found her too uppity for their personal comfort.

Carl had taken a second job off the farm at the rural lumber mill that kept him away from home even later. Malinda accepted this fact even as she waited inconsolably. To assist with household expenses Carl worked afternoons when farm chores were done. He was skilled at estimating lumber measurements and could calculate how many boards would make a barn frame, or a cross beam to support a roof. He even gained a surveyor's knowledge for setting a house of such and such dimensions and would help locals with building plans. This would profit his endeavors later.

Where was her tardy husband? Malinda pined for Carl to return when she and little John so needed him now? Sadly, her husband was not heading home. He had tried earnestly to tell her the previous day. No, he had an army to join. And he was on his way on his horse to the location where inductees were enlisted, the DeKalb City Hall.

Carl saddles his white stallion King for new adventures in the Union Army.

Carl Enlists in 1st Illinois Union Engineers

Induction records record that William Carl Hatcher enlisted in the Union Army on 20 January 1864 as a private. He arrived at the induction office located in DeKalb's City Hall and filled out the papers presented to him. His big white stallion horse, King, waited patiently outside for Carl to fulfill his public duty. He was already reading through the declarations and affixed his name at the bottom of the government document. All was signed, sealed and confirmed.

Carl quickly donned the uniform that was entrusted to him by a friend serving as quartermaster for entering volunteers. The regulation blue trousers and chasseur blouse fitted reasonably well as did the enlisted man's kepi (military cap). His 1842 rifled musket and assigned equipment were of standard design and quality. This included his Brogan shoes, a soft knapsack and sack coat (overcoat), all in good condition. He accepted it as standard equipment and of good quality for an enlisted man.

Private (Pvt.) Carl Hatcher was assigned to the 1st Illinois Union Engineers and joined his unit 28 January 1864. He gained access to the prestigious corps that was usually reserved for graduates of the U.S. Military Academy. West Point cadets who finished at the head of their class were appointed to the Army Corps of Engineers. In effect, Private Carl Hatcher joined an outfit where learning to construct bridges and build the strongest possible fortifications were of the highest priority for the Federal Army.

The engineer officer in the Corps of Engineers was always one of the most valued on any commander's staff, advising on topography and preferred avenues of advance. Carl meshed in this unit with his lumberman skill and surveyor's knowledge. Besides, he was highly commended by his uncle, Raymond Hatcher, whose influence was well known in the community. He and his mount, King, had papers properly signed and checked. Then Carl proudly rode off to join his unit as they awaited orders for entry into the war.

His select assignment gained him placement as kind of an unofficial "aide de camp"—a military advisor assisting a superior officer. He was assigned under Colonel Miles Randall of the 1st Illinois Union Engineers and Mechanics. A stoutly built West Pointer, Randall was injured by shrapnel at the 1861 Confederate attack on Fort Sumner and limped slightly. While the colonel ran a tight ship according to fellow officers, his enlisted soldiers respected Randall's grasp of engineers and mechanics and what they could perform in military situations. Carl was of similar disposition in respect for the astute-minded colonel.

Pvt. Hatcher gained respect from his superiors, including Cpt. Samuel Hornblower, his immediate supervisor. A strikingly handsome officer with West Point credentials, he wore deep sideburns and was known as fair but allowed no straying from the battalion's motto, "Build the best for the best." Pvt. Hatcher's noncommissioned position gave him supervisory control over an engineer's construction crew. In this role he saw action constructing union fortifications and building horse corrals and shelters for his soldiers always near rear combat areas. Carl would eventually experience involvement in major battles from Shiloh to the Battle of Atlanta and Sherman's laying waste to the South.

Every time a general needed someone to supervise the lumber mill or construct defensive fortifications, "Aide de Camp" Pvt. Hatcher was sent to that location. He served under the commands of General George Meade, General Ulysses S. Grant and even under the hesitant General George McClellan. The latter failed to follow up his tactical advantage by allowing Confederate General Robert E. Lee's troops to escape a possible defeat at Antietam.

Moving into 1865 Carl found his way to the command of General William Tecumseh Sherman. Sherman was a brilliant military commander, businessman, educator and author. He was designated by general Commander of Union troops, General Grant, to assume command of the western theater of the war. Further charged by Grant to plan a southern advance, Sherman executed a military campaign that included the capture of Atlanta on November 15, 1864. From there his command left a wide swath of destruction and pillage from Atlanta to Savannah on the coast of Georgia. His battle plan was to destroy both the South's war-making industries and the will and support of the civilian population. He was revered in the North but reviled in the South for years to come due to the psychological warfare he introduced.

Carl's combat action and the reason for his promotion to higher rank was due to a mysterious cannon ball firing. After constructing wood corrals for the 3rd New Jersey Calvary, Carl had retired to his tent. Outside, his men worked at a conveyor belt carrying wood planks to the coal-engine operated saw. Working in the calm of a cool fall day, the soldiers were hard at their arduous task. Pvt. Hatcher had trained them well.

Suddenly a violent rush of air caused Carl to respond tensely along with his men. The unexpected cannon ball, exploding from the barrel due to a faulty firing fuse, sped across the sky and erupted over the lumber mill. The sudden shock of the explosion set the coal engine on fire and alerted the soldiers to fiery danger. Carl quickly kicked in his farm agility, jumping through the flames to rescue two soldiers trapped beneath the burning planks. Pulling one man to his feet and pushing him to a safe distance, Carl carried the second soldier to safety outside the ring of flames.

The smaller private sustained 2nd degree burns on his shoulder and back, the larger soldier was luckier. He broke an ankle as Carl pulled him from beneath a heavy piece of oak. Both men owed their lives to the quick reaction of their supervisor. How the canon ball was inside the cannon barrel in the first place for firing remains a mystery.

Carl's heroics under fire earned him the Union Army recognition of Valor. He would forever cherish the tri-colored ribbon with oak leaf cluster embellishing the top. He thereby gained the rank of Corporal (Cpl.), wearing double-chevrons on his right sleeve. His rank raised him to a noncommissioned "officer who keeps order" and put him in charge of a squad of 11 soldiers. The corporal would oversee and set the standard for his new command's military conduct as engineers and mechanics.

General Sherman's sweep through the already depleted southern states led ultimately to the April 9, 1865 end of the Civil War. Two old adversaries met at Appomattox Court House, Virginia as Union commander General Grant accepted the surrender of Confederate General Lee. The war had ended, and Cpl. Carl Hatcher had not only the recognition of valor medal but major experience in building field fortifications, river pontoons and livestock enclosures. The Corps of Engineers had played an important part in the Union's victory and Carl was part of that accomplishment.

Corporal Hatcher receives fresh orders
from unit commander Colonel Miles Randall.

Corporal Hatcher Continues Building Assignment

Carl's fortunes found him in southern territory with no Union fortifications to construct, no bridges or forts to design. He decided to approach his commanding officer to ask what was next in his military service. What was his next assignment and where would it be?

Arriving at Col. Miles Randall's tent, Carl found him seated and alone with his writing journal open before him. Randall motioned Hatcher to sit down across the table from him. Carl declined, thinking it would be discourteous to sit before his commanding officer. He much preferred to stand while asking what a noncommissioned officer who had amassed his skills should do now that the war had ended.

"Sir, I served proudly over the past year with the Corps. I am here to request if an assignment that makes use of my experience is available at this time?"

"Just what is your hesitancy in exploring work in this area of the South?" Col. Randall asked. "Many challenges face southerners in this very area."

"I am afraid, Sir," Carl summoned his resolve, "that my engineer's career is sadly closed in this part of the country. My recent assignment with Gen. Sherman identifies me with his destructive march through the South. That is a great deal to forgive, Sir," the corporal stated as if it were common knowledge.

"Corporal, you have served the Union well and deserve the army commendation you received by your brave actions. I recently received requests for Union soldiers qualified in construction to assist southerners restore buildings, roads and bridges in their scarred fields. I see no reason why you would not be a good choice to handle such requests?" Col. Randall probed.

"This is regardless of your past record with General Sherman. You were merely carrying out your engineer instructions. The regrettable war is now over. Are you available for these requests? Your work would be sufficiently rewarded by respect if not available cash."

"Yes sir," exclaimed Carl determinedly. "Anything to offer help to those in need."

Cpl. Hatcher was thankful his past connection with the destructive campaign was seemingly forgotten. Col. Randall had granted permission to the corporal who was young in years but long in experience. He could act on requests to help southern land owners and in that way help the South, which was surprising. Nevertheless, Carl would work in the rebuilding process with his engineer's squad and use the squad's horses for transport as needed.

Combat engineer Hatcher joins in reconstruction efforts of Southern States.

Hatcher Joins in Reconstruction

Soon after receiving his orders, Cpl. Hatcher put aside plans for a return to northern territory. First, he followed up on his decision to grow facial hair since he would work outside Union Army regulations. Next, he would dedicate himself to meeting the urgent request from discouraged citizens beginning in Georgia. Cpl. Hatcher would be part of the complex Reconstruction of the South. It was during this time that the corporal became interested in southern history. Learning the date a state entered the Union was essential to his knowledge of the state's present history. He could share this information with those he worked to aid as a serious student of southern culture. Nevertheless, he was sorry to acknowledge these same states left the U.S. as secessionists in 1861. Nothing he could do now, Carl reasoned, except to help these same war-weary states recover.

Georgia was the starting place. It became the fourth state in 1788 and was known as a cotton-growing slave state. Carl was asked to rebuild barns and shattered fences, infrastructure for cotton gins and restore rail lines. This was fully approved by his higher command with the war concluded. The remaining time of the corporal's military service was to act more like a civilian. His experience was to be put to good use, responding to requests to help rebuild the very South he had previously been an agent in destroying.

Carl's journey of rebuilding barns and resituating rail lines increased as he traveled along the coastline away from Georgia. Southerners, not surprisingly, were still in shock and wondered if their current lives and the culture that supplied such comfort to them formerly could continue. The agrarian South could not survive economically with no slaves to work the fields. Lincoln's acts to abolish slavery had real meaning to southern land owners. Chaos was the order of the day, and Congress labored with the input of local and sectional leaders to restore the Union as a united government that all could honor and respect.

This was the time that Carpetbaggers came in number as opportunists from the North to promote not always positive ties. Meanwhile, white southern Unionists or "scalawags" came to establish self-serving roles in lining their own pockets with southern cash. Carl was able to work around most of these, but he butted heads more often than he wanted with northern interlopers. At every stop, however, he found southerners willing to work alongside his squad on reconstruction projects.

Next state along the coast was Florida. It was admitted to the union as a slave state in 1845 but joined the Confederacy at the start of the Civil War. The state seemed to have escaped major damage from the war, so Carl found jobs installing bridges and protective walls for citrus tree groves. Next, Alabama a slave state, entered the

Union in 1819 but withdrew from the Union in 1861. It was home to the first capital of the Confederacy, Montgomery. After the war the state was developing its entry in the steel industry and required its infrastructure rebuilt to accomplish the beginning phases.

One of its residents was a hardy woman named Mildred "Pepper" Farmer. Carl developed a convivial friendship with the quirky, brown-haired lady. Her last name seemed to suit her and reminded him of home. "Salt and Pepper" was the nickname the 53-year-old Ms. Farmer gained for her graying temples. She worked tirelessly, wearing a denim dress and jacket with red bandana to meetings with important business leaders. Her goal was to meet with as many statewide businesses owners as possible, encouraging them to provide land for the large buildings needed to house industrial production.

Having meals together, Carl and Pepper shared their thoughts on the work each was trying to accomplish. Their efforts merged in opening opportunities for contributing to the rebuilding the "Heart of Dixie". When they broke for lunch, Carl's squad began calling them "the double-trouble duo".

"I admire your persistence, Pepper," Carl stated. "You seem to know most of the Alabama businessmen, or at least those who are active in business."

"Let's just say I'm lucky knowing the ones who still have money," replied Pepper. "It's hard to know who still continues in a reputable business."

"What do you mean by 'reputable?'" Carl asked.

"Oh, you know, the ones who still have a 'legal' label behind their business name. So many business leaders in the state are selling out to Carpetbaggers. Together they pursue private gain by taking advantage of unsettled conditions and political corruption."

"Must make finding the good ones to deal with a tough sell, huh? My reconstruction efforts are a little easier. Only the ones who have money to invest are in position to ask my crew to work with them," Carl explained.

Pepper agreed, and they ate their lunch quietly with Carl surmising the older woman had a lot of good in her venture. Her work to insist Alabama businessmen promote the state by promising land investment was a worthy but ambitious cause given the present circumstances. He wished Pepper Farmer good luck in her journey across the state.

Mississippi was Carl's next stop. It became a state in 1817 and joined the Confederacy in 1861. It was the southern state that suffered most from important battles waged within its borders. General Grant won the decisive battle of Vicksburg that gave the Union control of the Mississippi River. Controlling that major Confederate transportation line further crippled the South's ability to support its struggling military. January 1865 brought an end to war but not the end of the state's civil rights struggles.

Racial discrimination was still prevalent in the state even after slavery was abolished with Lincoln's Emancipation Proclamation issued January 1, 1863. It essentially allowed slaves freedom in the states rebelling against the Union; Federal troops occupying secessionist states could legally free slaves they came upon. Later the 13th Amendment ratified by Congress on December 8, 1865 further abolished slavery in the United States. States like Mississippi did not liberate slaves easily and this led to further mishandling of the US Congressional mandates.

One such example of just plain ignorance involved Jonathan McGinty. Mr. McGinty lost his plantation and family home in Alabama but was able to relocate in southern Mississippi where he had family. He managed to accrue enough capital to purchase land north of New Orleans, bringing with him a single slave. Contracting with Carl's team of engineers to construct a new barn, McGinty continually berated and swore at the male slave as the barn was raised. Carl could only watch as the southerner verbally assaulted the damaged and unappreciated young man. The relocated southern property owner still had legal ownership of the treated slave, and Carl had to bite his tongue to avoid butting in. He could only hope that the handsome young slave would one day be granted freedom and allowed to relocate with his family as he could. President Lincoln's Thirteenth Amendment that was ratified that year would certainly make that possibility a reality.

At last, Carl entered the state of Louisiana. It gained statehood in 1812 through partition of the Louisiana Purchase in creating states. The state's northern tier was recognized as free and the south as slave. New Orleans was the largest city in the south and the 6th largest in the United States. It was a city captured by Union ships in 1861 with the surrender of Fort Jackson.

Rebuilding and bridge construction in mid-1860s were restarting in the state that carried the mighty Mississippi and a host of smaller rivers. Numerous reconstruction projects retained Carl's business skills as he sought to reach New Orleans. His commanding officer, Col Randall, advised before he would depart for his home in Pennsylvania, that New Orleans would be Carl's mustering out site. With the colonel's departure with his unit, Carl was left without a squad to command. The tired and homesick soldiers were leaving on their northward journeys home.

The historic city of New Orleans was Carl's last stop in August 1865. He had advisement that he would complete his volunteer service there but was surprised at the location. He was officially discharged with Distinguished Service from the Union Army on 20 August 1865, following 18 months of military service. His loyalty to the 1st Illinois Engineers Corps and further service in southern states reconstruction found him at age 27 a good distance from home.

All through his enlistment, Carl had maintained a weekly telegram correspondence with his family in DeKalb. Unbeknown to Carl, his aggrieved wife had never opened any of his messages but destroyed them as soon as they got into her hands. Also unknown to the "prodigal husband" was the sad story of Malinda and their two sons at the family home in DeKalb, Illinois.

Jurgens Hench overhears Malinda's virulent complaints against Union Army's successes as he works at DeKalb telegraph office.

Malinda Fosters Own Misery

After Carl departed home to join the Union Army, Malinda continued her vehement complaints against the Union's "barbaric actions." Especially defending the plight of her former state Tennessee, she disavowed "reported victories" of the North at the disastrous battle of Shiloh in 1862 and the later Chattanooga bloodbath. So loud was her spiteful indignation that she angered the feelings of some residents of her home area.

Especially injured by Malinda Lee Hatcher's constant haranguing was the DeKalb telegraph office located at the court house. Telegraph operator was Jurgens Hench. Use of the telegraph was not overly expensive, and the existing commercial telegraph network was well used by the Union military for sending important messages. The United

States Military Telegraph (USMT) War Department utilized the civilian service almost exclusively for sending all levels of messages. For unknown reasons, Confederate officials failed to make as good use of the telegraph network.

Malinda went regularly to collect telegrams from her parents in Chicago. Operator Jurgens Hench could not help but overhear her continuing, self-gratifying complaints. Later, he learned that her father, Thomas Mason, was an assertive Confederate. The elder Mason would come to visit his daughter and was often sent to collect telegraphed messages sent by wife Deedee from Chicago.

"You don't know the wounds we have to suffer," Mr. Mason exclaimed to a man present to collect his own messages. "Our troops are beaten down and trodden under Union army oppression. Oh, that the clamor over a family owning a few slaves should promote a ridiculous war like this! 'Tis a mystery to me."

"Hmm," muttered Jurgens Hench as he stood behind the telegraph counter, "that visitor to town has his own ridiculous ideas. To complain about this awful war is a thing the South started anyway." Now he could hardly wait to tell other friends what he had just overheard.

"Neil," he hailed his bewhiskered-friend on the street outside the hardware store, "that city fellow from Chicago just grumbled about the slavery concern. He even talked about how the North's causing it." Hench related the Mason conversation with just a bit of rearranging.

"Say," Neil rejoined, "isn't that the same rant we've heard from that Malinda Hatch who keeps telling everyone who'll listen she used to be from Tennessee?"

"Yeah, he's the father of her'n and a southern sympathizer for sure," said Hench, as a crowd gathered to learn what the loud talking was about.

"You know what we do with those kinds of people who have kinship with the South," put in Ira Stout, a short gentleman from down the street.

"No," intoned Henry Limber, "what do we do with folks like that?"

"Why, we send 'em out of town," said Stout. "We don't abide them in the North for their contrary ideas!"

"You know," Hench said, "Malinda's husband left for the Union army some time ago. No one knows when a volunteer like him will return. Why don't we show Malinda Hatcher just what the citizens of our fair city think of her? By golly, her constant bickering about southern ways should not go unanswered."

"Agreed," the gathered men exclaimed. And they set out to scare Malinda with a small fire out by her wood shed. They reasoned that should scare her enough to think about leaving the town.

Mysterious fire destroys Hatcher house as Jurgens Hench observes.
Only one of five men present knows full story.

Fiery Attack on the Hatcher House

Just after sundown the self-aroused vigilante crowd of five men approached the Hatcher house on the corner of Sycamore and Lane streets. Carrying a lantern and kerosene, Stout asked Horace Limber to spill the kerosene across the bottom plank of the woodshed door.

"Be careful with where you spread the 'sene. You want it just on the shed door. We don't want to catch any of the wood inside on fire. Burning the door off'n the shed will scare little Miss Hatcher enough she may be inclined to leave for good."

"Right," said Limber as he proceeded to spread the flammable liquid on the outside of the door before Stout offered a rag he was carrying. Carefully opening the glass covering on the lantern, he lighted the cloth and dropped the rag on the doused door. A quick flame ensued, and the men moved back.

Unknown to the vigilantes, an open oil can was just inside the door. Unsuspecting and unknowing, Malinda had not closed the oil can. Her husband had brought it home to store in the outside shed from lumber mill use. That was mistake number one.

Mistake number two was when a giant puff of wind rose up. The now flaming shed door fell inward, exploding the oil can. Suddenly what the men had planned for only a small blaze turned into a fiery inferno. The outside shed and wood inside sparked the flame that spread to the roof of the house. Mistake number three: the house caught the blaze, and it looked to the gathered men that all was lost.

Coincidentally, most of the men were on the volunteer fire department. By the time they returned to the fire hall and brought back the fire trailer, the house was embroiled in fierce flames. It was later declared a complete loss by Jurgens Hench, who served as the local fire marshal.

Good fortune had Malinda and the two boys visiting overnight at her parent's home in Chicago. Under the circumstances, they were not to return to DeKalb. Her father saw to that upon hearing anonymously from one of the men present at the fire that destroyed the home. Only a fire-darkened slab remained, and that was covered by burnt timbers and scattered family belongings, he was told.

The anonymous informant was Homer Justice. He would later move to Chicago and did not want the Masons to learn his identity. He in no way took credit for his silent involvement in the fire that burned the Hatcher home. The truth he held would be his alone to tell at the proper time.

Telegraph operator Jurgens Hench died soon after the incineration of the home of a heart attack. He took leadership of the loosely organized group with him to the grave. The other men involved in the

46

plot vowed never to talk about the fire that went terribly wrong. No loose talk, no conversation. No mention of the ill-fated fire topic whatsoever.

What happened to the Mason family was a tale of woe and relocation. After the fire consumed the Hatcher house, Thomas Mason moved his family south again. He took wife Deedee, older daughter Malinda Lee and younger sister Savannah, now married and living with George Pierce in Chicago, as the family relocated to Memphis. This move took them to far southwest Tennessee and to Memphis, which was probably one of the least damaged cities in the state. Malinda Lee, of course, left Illinois with no forwarding address.

Suffice it to say, few knew what happened to the family who lived in the house destroyed by the mysterious fire. The name Hatcher lived on only in the minds of those who caused the fire. Oh, a few from church recalled her and those "sweet little boys," but they assumed Malinda had moved the family when "that terrible fire" consumed her home.

Meanwhile Malinda, now resettled in Tennessee, received advice from her concerned father. "Daughter Malinda, I want to advise you," spoke Mr. Mason as he appeared to be wise but in effect started a family myth that would perpetuate itself over the years.

"I suggest you tell folks that your husband left you one night and did not return. He deserted you and the boys in a drunken rage; he abandoned you and never returned." Mr. Mason continued, "It would not go well to say he joined the army and fought with the Union side. That could raise some southern ire and surely lead to embarrassing questions in our new residence."

"Father, I suppose you are right," sadly affirmed Malinda.

"You'll see it will be better in the long run. From now on your former husband does not exist," he exclaimed with finality.

"You will need to pass this teaching on to John and Willis to ensure they realize their father will not return—ever. I also think it would be good that you do not allow any pictures or personal effects of Carl's to appear around the house," Thomas advised.

"I do not wish to damage the family name either, Father. However, I will always have good memories for the warmth and caring Carl gave me. We had five years together before he left. I will remember him for the good husband he was and father to our sons." (Still the thought persisted that Carl had chosen the army over her. And what kind of husband did that make him, really?)

With that, the father and daughter joined the rest of the family in a pact of allegiance that Malinda's husband indeed abandoned his family. He was an alcoholic who probably was in such a stupor he could not even remember where home was!

Civilian Carl buys shoulder bag from "Dusty" Towner,
a former Confederate soldier, at New Orleans Port.

Civilian Carl Travels Mississippi River

Now a civilian with no military connection, Carl William Hatcher turned his attention to finding his way home. He had continued hope his wife and sons had survived the war. He could only surmise his family had lost the means to respond to him. Had they perished in the guerrilla wars that raged across the prairies? Did his wife's southern sympathies bring her harm? What happened to his small family in Illinois?

He felt he had lost the love of his life, sweet, pretty Malinda Lee, and his two young sons as well." *What were their names? John and Willie, no Willis.* "What happened to them?"

The telegraph he hurriedly dispatched from New Orleans to his Illinois home gained no reply. Perhaps Carl should expect nothing

Rev. Jerry Heydenberk

less. His family was gone. Would he never have the experience of being a husband, a father again?

Carl packed his duffel bag and looked over the train schedule. There were no trains. Too much rail bed damage. Go to river transport. He noted that the *John Kilgore* steamboat was scheduled to make its first travel from New Orleans to St. Louis, Missouri, second largest port in the country. The Mississippi at times was cruel to careless pilots along its 1,200 miles. Many flatboats of the period were swept off course, waylaid by the "Father of Waters." They would pile up on a sandbar or be swept downstream by the swift currents. Carl's trip was not to be filled with such adventures.

The next morning he would make provisions for his horse King to be sheltered below deck. He imagined his steed would not like the dark, windowless space to which he would be haltered for the 29-hour trip. Reluctantly, Carl would bid King goodbye with the promise he would take his horse out of the cramped stall after they made port in St. Louis.

Carl had enough funds from before his mustering out process to pay 1st class passage on the steamboat. He readied himself by carefully packing his knapsack after scouring the shops on Canal Street for a bigger shoulder bag for packing his personal items.

"Wish I had a larger bag to pack in," Carl said unconsciously but loud enough to hear. He found the small, soft knapsack issued him by the Union Army ample but not ample enough for all his personal effects.

"Pardon me, but I could not help overhear your plea for a bigger luggage bag," a stranger interrupted. "I picked up a good-sized shoulder bag in my final year with the Confederacy and would sell it to you. I plan on staying in New Orleans, a real party and music town, for a good while."

Carl found it interesting to carry on a conversation with a former Confederate soldier, especially one who was black and wore civilian clothes as he did. The man also seemed to have better equipment than he had during his Union days.

"Why, that would be a good sale," responded Carl. "I am to leave on a steamboat tomorrow and need a larger bag for my packing needs. What would you be asking for the shoulder bag?"

"That's a good question," said the black man. "Didn't cost me none since it 'twas part of my army supply. How 'bout two dollars. You think that's 'nough?"

"Yes, that's more than fair," Carl agreed. The two then exchanged first, money passed one way and the purchased bag the other, then fascinating conversation. Carl learned the Confederate soldier, "Dusty" Towner, was a former member of the 8th Texas Calvary, "Terry's Texas Rangers,' C.S.A. (Confederate States of America). The Rangers were one of the toughest mounted outfits of the Confederate Army, recruited from Texans who had fought Indians, Mexicans and free-staters for years. The Civil War duty was just a carry-on of their work.

They rode into battle under a distinctive banner that carried the regiment's name and the motto, "God Defends the Right." Carl thought this amusing as he thought God defended his troops as the rightful protectors of the Union. He also found it interesting that the Rangers carried a Colt revolver rather than a sword. Towner explained to Carl that most cavalrymen had a disdain for the sabre and preferred a sidearm instead.

Boarding the steamboat the following morning, Carl wondered if his fellow passengers would be of the same good nature he met in Dusty Towner. He did not have long to wait for the answer. Walking to the rail to watch the giant paddle wheels turn rapidly in propelling the steamer forward, Carl came across a young black girl. She appeared about the age of 10 or 11, he thought, as he complimented the colorful head scarf atop her coal black hair.

"Hallo, Miss, you certainly have a colorful scarf, just the fashion of New Orleans."

"Why mistah," the girl looked up from her souvenir book, *New Orleans Today*, "I find your words nice and particularly meaningful."

Her mother approached walking toward him. She was wearing a brightly colored head scarf as well and a bright yellow dress of ankle length. She was big-boned and smiling broadly.

"Hello, I see you've met my busy daughter," the woman greeted. "She is always reading, and looking for someone to talk to."

"Quite a young lady," Carl replied. "Just the two of you traveling to . . . ?" and he left the destination unfinished waiting for her response.

"Why, mercy no. We have a large family traveling. We are going to St. Louis to meet friends of Harriet Tubman, all 8 of us."

Carl remembered the name of the woman who had used the Underground Railroad as a network to rescue enslaved people. Born Arminta Ross about 1822 (slaves were given no birth certificates), she started working with the Union Army as a cook and nurse, then became an armed scout and spy. It was reported she rescued some 70 people, including her family and friends to escape into free states and Canada. She worked with the aid of abolitionists both black and white. To meet people who knew of this courageous woman was like finding a treasure hidden in a field for someone to chance upon. Now he was about to know where the treasure was hidden.

"You say you are friends of Harriet Tubman, the woman who worked to free escaping slaves?" Carl asked, then added, "My name is Carl Hatcher and I am just returning home from engineers' duty with the Union Army."

"Oh my, a real hero, I must say," she exclaimed. "Let me introduce myself. I'm Sassy Fields and my daughter is Georgia. Her father, my husband, Moses, is a freed-slave that Harriet Tubman saved three months ago. We are traveling to rejoin him."

"You say you are meeting friends of Harriet Tubman?" Carl continued the conversation.

"Yes," answered Sassy, "Moses and a friend are meeting us. They have so much respect for this wonderful woman who rescued my husband. Missus Tubman was able to persuade his former owners, abolitionists themselves, to get Moses to the Underground Railroad. That was in Maryland where he had been sold and made the tedious journey from slave owner to slave owner away from his home in New Orleans.

"And listen to what Moses told me," Sassy rejoined. "This tells about Missus Tubman's confidence in working to set these slaves free. Moses said she boasted once, 'I was conductor of the Underground Railroad for eight years, and I can say what most conductors can't say—I never ran my train off the track and I never lost a passenger.'"

"What an amazing thing to remember," said Carl. "Your husband must be much indebted to such a special lady." Carl was grateful for meeting this black woman and would look forward to conversations with her family. He wanted to learn as much as he could about freed-slaves and their new status as freed men who would in time be given their citizenship.

What a nice way to begin his journey to St. Louis. He would find transport the rest of the distance to Chicago and certainly some new people to visit with. And from there to DeKalb, and what would he find of his family there? He could only hope they would be unharmed and ready to meet him.

Dino, your pizzeria is great for food and service.
Wish I could feed King pizza to thank him for his hard work.

Continuing Journey Home to Illinois

Again, Carl Hatcher had to wonder why his discharge point had to be New Orleans in the deep south. He entered volunteer service at the DeKalb City Hall in Illinois and listed that as his home of record. What made the Federal Army headquarters consider this long trek home worthy of his honorable military service? Well, the army had its own concept of travel, Carl figured. Of course, he would receive no reimbursement for transportation costs for the long journey from New Orleans through St. Louis.

Arriving at the St. Louis docks comfortably the following day, Carl retrieved his horse from below deck, took his duffel bag and backpack and began to plan how to make the final leg of his journey. He wandered the docks to inquire if another steamboat was heading north with a Chicago port of destination. He found nothing was scheduled before the next month. As this was the close of August, he was told the waterway passages up the Mississippi were unpredictable due to summer flooding and that steamboats were susceptible to running aground on barely submerged sandbars. This seemed plausible enough to Carl except he needed a rapid return home.

Meantime he decided to rent himself and his horse out for labor needs around the dock. Eventually referred to a small factory delivery service, Carl was offered employment to load and pick up passenger's private baggage for delivery to local hotels. After a time spent in deciding, he accepted the labor-intensive offer and was hired with King to carry out the delivery service.

Carl's new boss, Floyd Bickel, assumed a supervisor's seniority at the start of the new man's employment, stating "You and your horse be careful when picking up baggage and offloading from the buckboard the company is only renting you. Your most diligent attention to detail is always expected. Do not overload or be careless of each piece you load."

Carl thanked Mr. Bickel for the information and admonition, thinking it was best to acquiesce to his supervisor's terse comments to retain the job he had just acquired. Next on the agenda was to find sleeping quarters for at least the next four days of his employment. He had success when an apartment over the livery stable where he would stable King became available. Cost, interestingly, was two dollars a day for his horse and two dollars for Carl. Carl was amused at the equal cost for himself and his horse, but the total expenses would be well covered by the four-day employment that would gain them $200.

Carl and King worked confidently as a team, which was the way it always was with the obedient and talented big white stallion. A horse that Carl weaned from the herd that his uncle, Raymond Hatcher, selected for him from his ranch in Illinois. Carl had broken the horse while King was still young and put his first bridle and saddle on him at 2 ½ years. Other training had the horse primed for grooming, leading, stable behavior and entering a horse trailer. King had mastered each teaching with poise and determination to make his master proud of him. Carl appreciated the fact that King had grown into a well-adjusted, handsome adult horse.

The two worked in tandem as master carefully loaded the buckboard with luggage items and horse carried the loaded wagon to various community hotels. There Carl inquired at the counter to know where each piece should be delivered to the exact hotel room. At day's end Carl and King took the empty buckboard to park at the livery where King was stabled for the night. Carl, meanwhile, took his evening meal at an Italian restaurant only two blocks away that served good food with amazingly efficient service. The manager, Dino Donatello, was gracious and much used to service veterans patronizing his St. Louis restaurant, Dino's Pizzeria. Although pizza did not appear on American menus until US soldiers brought the doughy food back from WWII service in Italy, early attempts of serving pizza in this country were limited but popular. Dino's in St. Louis was one example. The manager inquired of Carl about his service and service connections. He then told him his own uncle, Antonio, served with a Confederate unit.

"Yes, it was my oldest uncle of the Donatello family, one Antonio. In Italian it means 'the blessed one.' I can assure you my uncle was a blessed one as he was a proud survivor of many skirmishes. The terrible Civil War that often pitted brother against brother and even father against son. Let me tell you that two of my uncles served on either side. A sad commentary on the war for our family."

"Do you recall his unit name?" Carl pursued the conversation one evening at Dino's.

"Why, I do not recall the unit name, but it was known as 'Terry's Texas Rangers.' Antonio claimed it was the hardest ridin' Calvary outfit of the war. They were active before war broke out with trained Texans of mixed color. I remember they carried pistols instead of sabers for weapons."

"What a coincidence," Carl rejoined, "why I heard about them from a fellow who sold me his shoulder bag. They were the 8th Texas Cavalry, as I recall. Did you ever hear of a black member of that unit named Dusty Towner?"

"I can't say that I do. My uncle didn't even tell me the name of the outfit's leader. All he said of the commander was that he was a real 'ornery critter and someone you didn't want to mess with after work."

"Just imagine that," Carl remarked. "You can't say the war didn't bring the strangest of people together in unexpected contacts." Dino agreed, and this set both men into thinking of stories they heard of Union soldiers attending to wounds of Confederates and vice versa.

Carl stands in shock outside white picket fence he had lovingly built to encircle his now burned out home.

Homeward Bound but Where is Home?

Finding a way out of St. Louis with no water passage open due to seasonal rains was no problem because rail transportation continued. Riding the train from that city on to Chicago was very reliable. Civil War battle damage extended many miles south of St. Louis; however, the northern railroad system was spared damage. Most rail lines had been destroyed in the southern states where Carl helped in reconstruction. Projects he remembered vividly whirled in his mind from rebuilding infrastructure such as livestock barns, industrial buildings and working to restore railroad lines.

Finding a passenger train with livestock car for King was not as easy as Carl first thought. He spent all of three days before he could book passage on a freight train bound to Chicago on the 29th of August

1865. Departure before the next morning's travel saw Carl spend extra dollars for further overnight lodging at the livery stable.

Train transportation took a little over six hours. Unloading King from one livestock car and reloading him onto another train took much of the time. Making the afternoon train connection to DeKalb and home was less than an hour's time. All the way Carl had mixed feelings as he traveled nearer to his home. He had left Malinda Lee and their two sons in the town home and it was there he would visit first. He had only the hope of long-carried memories that he would soon be re-united with his family. The farmstead he would check soon enough.

When Carl arrived at the corner of Sycamore and Lane Streets, he was greeted by the unthinkable. Sadly, Carl Hatcher surveyed what was left of his home. Only charred ruins and blackened posts re-mained where the two-story house had stood. The shed behind the house had completely deteriorated as if an explosion had erased every fragment into spent ashes.

Where could he find out about his wife and sons? Who would know whether they survived the fire that destroyed his home? Tragedy cannot always be kept in one place. For Carl the horror of what he might find was unthinkable. A slow, agonizing death? Serious burns? Mother separated from sons? It was almost more than he could grasp. Oh, the number of possibilities was unthinkable.

Carl had to start his search somewhere. He thought and wondered where someone would know what happened at this now empty lot. In a city that hosted presidential candidate Abraham Lincoln only four years previously, Carl was devastated. And now that great states-man Lincoln was dead, killed by the bullet from the gun of a despon-dent actor and Confederate sympathizer. It was as if Carl could now focus all his pent up emotions at the assassin. *Oh, that mean little man, his actions mirror my sorrow and loss right now. How I would like to be able to banish that scoundrel from the face of the earth!*

A passerby stopped as Carl sadly surveyed the wreckage of his home. "What happened to that house is catastrophic," the town librarian, Harriet Main exclaimed. "Did you know someone who lived there?"

Carl stopped his fuming long enough to regain composure and answered, "I am looking for the family who lived here. A young mother and two boys. They were my family and I am here trying to find what happened to them," he said with anguish.

"I might suggest," said Mrs. Main, "that checking with the local telegraph office might be a place to start. The operator may have a record of telegrams that could help you learn something of your family. The young man there may be of some help to you," she offered helpfully.

"And where is the office? I have been away for some time and need some directions, please."

"It just moved. It was on the bottom floor of the court house but is now located in a small building next to the bank. Just there to your right," and she pointed down the street. Carl thanked the woman for her help and turned away from the hapless ruin of what was an active home.

When Carl came to the town's telegraph office, he was on a mission. He desperately needed to find if anyone could tell him where his wife and sons had gone. Walking in the door, Carl noted the operator bent over the telegraph and rapidly jotting down a message. He sat down to wait on one of the straight back chairs. Next to the partially open window, the waiting room can hold only three or four customers. The little building had a smoked-in smell that seemed to extend through the open door as he entered. As he continued to wait for the operator to cease his work, Carl noted a small pile of cigarette stubs on the table next to a premature bald man. Standing as tall as he could, Carl faced the seated man and readied to ask his much-rehearsed question.

"Sir, I'm looking for any information you may have about my missing wife and two sons. Malinda Hatcher and boys John and Willis. They lived in the house that was burned on the corner of Sycamore and Lane Streets," Carl attempted to sound hopeful that the young man would be able to help. The operator was bespectacled and wore suspenders pulling up his striped trousers over a round tummy. What a funny little man, Carl could not help thinking to himself. The bald man's stooped posture and nervous manner were clear indications he was new at his work.

"I am so sorry, sir," the telegraph operator rejoined. "My name is Ira Pound, and I am new here. The previous operator, a Mr. Hench, died of a heart attack just after leaving the office one night about three weeks ago." This was a real blow to Carl's search through this office.

"But have you received any telegrams from me from New Orleans," an exasperated Carl asked. "From me, Carl William Hatcher. It would've been sent August 20th, this month."

"I am sorry, sir. Mr. Hench's records he took home with him that night. Unfortunately, the missing telegrams have not been found to date." *What kind of office efficiency is this? Why are all these blocks hurled at me in the search for my missing family?*

Carl's patience exceeded his respect for the young man's lack of knowledge. "Mr. Pound, do you not keep a record of all telegrams sent and those received at this office? Surely this office would have a record of all incoming and outgoing messages," he finished in despair.

"I'm sorry. I have told you all I know. Now, please let me wait on the young lady who is in the door behind you." Shifting his gaze to the doorway, he bid a greeting to the new customer.

"Hello, Miss Briant, what is my favor to help you with today? Is your father in need of a message to send today?"

"No, as to my father's need," the young lady stated. "I overheard the man who lost his family and is in obvious need of help in finding them. Mr. Hatcher, as I heard your name announced, is there something I or my father can do?"

The lady explained that her name was Chantel Briant. She said she was the daughter of the local pastor, Parson Cort Briant. They were from France and her father had recently taken the parish leadership for the Beacon Light Baptist Church in town. They were just removed from boat and train travel to this location and settled here.

"Oh, Miss Chantel," Carl thought immediately how she reminded him of auburn-haired Malinda Lee. They were about the same height, and this lady had a similar charming manner and fashionable dress. She had a confidence and vibrancy he had seldom seen in any woman.

"Excuse me, ma'am. Your offer is what my weary ears are ready to hear. But how do you think you can help after being in this city such a short time," stated Carl. "I left home nary a year passed and my family was alive and living in the house that is now completely gone."

"Shhh," said Chantel as she motioned Carl outside and away from the prying ears of Mr. Pound. Never one to be shy, she took Carl's hand and led him outside. They stopped a distance from the building.

"Now, Mr. Hatcher," Chantel tried to sound sympathetic in addressing the troubled man in front of her. "Even though my father and I have resided in DeKalb a short time, I can assure you my father is already well known in the community. He has called in homes and knows quite a few people through visits he makes with me tagging along. With a sigh, Chantel told of the home visits she was called to make with the parson to avoid any loose talk or malicious rumors.

Carl took in all this information. Even with experience in the so-called southern Bible Belt, he had not entered a church door in the past year. He did only because Malinda urged him to take the family. *How did one address a man of faith anyway?*

"Now, let's start on finding your family," Chantel interrupted him. "Did they have any relatives that you can contact, anyone that lives close by?"

Carl had indeed forgotten about the Masons, Malinda's parents. They had not crossed his mind in his haste to return home. Now he remembered that her parents lived only 40 miles away in Chicago. He did not realize their water crossings almost intersected. His recent river passage from New Orleans took him to St. Louis as the Mason family accomplished their travel downstream from Chicago to Memphis. His travel had just ended, theirs commenced some time previously. Thomas Mason wanted to get his family away from Illinois and the fire that caused the house burning as soon as possible.

"Why yes," muttered Carl. "My wife had her family living in Chicago." He had not carried a good feeling about Thomas and Deedee's influence on his wife since their wedding vows. Malinda's always seeming to throw up the family's heritage and slave ownership in Nashville were arguments he could not overcome. Those former years had turned his wife's flighty emotions directly toward the Confederate cause.

"Well, let's start there then," Chantel proclaimed confidently. "Perhaps we shall find out some clue as to their whereabouts."

Carl was so entranced by the take-charge behavior of the strange woman that he did not realize they had approached the telegram building again. He did realize the bright Chantel reminded him of the clever woman detective he read about in an engrossing article on his train ride from St. Louis. It was titled "Skilled Woman Solves Mysterious Clues." The story followed the female detective on her clever untangling of clues leading toward a suspicious nighttime murder. Carl found it difficult at this point to separate the smart literary character from the pastor's daughter-turned detective, Chantel. While he was thinking of the comparison, he realized she had grabbed his hand again and was pulling him forward.

"Where are you leading me now?" he stammered as they turned in the door of the telegraph office again and confronted the bald telegraph operator at his smelly table.

"Trust your instincts, Mr. Hatcher," Chantel countered. "You must send a telegraph to the relatives of your wife you mentioned live in Chicago. Do you have the address?"

"I hope I do," Carl mumbled, as he tried to jump his memory from all the reconstruction orders he received to the present time. "Wait, I think my memory is kicking in," he said as he remembered walking his future wife home years ago." Yes, I believe this is their address," as he quickly wrote down the requested street address.

"There," he said to the bald-headed man at the counter and handed him the paper, "This is the address I recall from visits to a Mason family in Chicago."

The telegram was soon sent to the operator on the other end. Carl paid the $1.75 cost as he and the young lady waited for the reply to this message.

Mason family 1521 Glendale Square Chicago stop.
trying to locate Malinda Hatcher of DeKalb. stop.
Have you any information? stop.
   Please inform at earliest convenience

Carl Hatcher

Sadly, there was no reply. Nothing. The telegraphed message was never answered. Where could this family have disappeared to? Why was his missing family such a frustrating and confusing puzzle? About that time, the young lady touched him on the arm to get his attention.

"Well, that's settled then," she breezed as if nothing was lost at all. "'Nothing attempted, nothing gained,' as my father would say.

Dear father, he is a bit of what you call over-protective. Since mother passed two years ago, pere has paid more attention to my life than necessary. He has such joy meeting people, getting to know them and then inviting them to church. His Sunday sermons and Wednesday night church meetings are usually well attended. And he always makes sure I am there as his obedient daughter. Sometimes I wonder if I have a father or a church parson eager to have my attendance at every possible service."

"Please, Miss Chantel, you are getting away from our main purpose—trying to find where my family has gone." Carl reminded the lady who was in the middle of reminisces that seemed more important to her than about their joined task. She was willing to help him but was also a person of much conversation, he thought.

"Oh, gracious," rejoined Chantel. "I forgot myself. When Maman Shantae passed, daddy had only me to care for. Sometimes he has his hands full, I must confess."

"Please, Miss Chantel," Carl attempted to steer her back to his interests again. "Do you have any more ideas about my family's whereabouts? I mean, what is our next plan?"

Carl, here is my pere' who is happy to meet you and has offered to help find your missing family.

Missing Family's Friends Questioned

At the very least Carl and his new "detective" friend now had the task of finding any person who might have known his wife and sons. They were literally "burned out of town," and Carl needed to find out why and for what reason. How would he go about it? In his current situation of unknowing, Carl had only Chantel to rely on for suggesting how to proceed.

A good detective takes advantage of all information that leads to helpful clues. Clue, meaning "a piece of evidence leading to the solution of a problem" and "to give reliable information to." Chantel was certainly worthy of following clues, Carl reasoned.

Very soon Chantel brought her father, Parson Cort Briant, to meet Carl. He was a small Frenchman who wore a plaid vest over pleated shirt and plain trousers. His hair was of the darkest black and he sported a little moustache above his upper lip. The parson was quite a genial person, Carl observed, as the two were introduced.

"Owi," the parson exclaimed. "It is my pleasure to meet you, Carl," and he pronounced the name with a decided French accent. "How can I be of help to you? My daughter assures me you have an important mission—to find your missing family. And she assures me she has an idea already how to solve the case."

Immediately, Carl recognized a similar phrasing from his reading in the smart detective woman article: she had clear vision on "how to solve the case." Indeed, mused Carl, these two people, one fictional and one reality, have identical ways of speaking. Imagine that.

"That's quite right, sir," as Carl did not know how to address a man of the cloth. Maybe he should tip his head, clasp his hands in prayer or at least bow.

"You can call me what you want, Carl, parson or pastor. *Cam 'est egal*, It's all the same to me."

Well, at least that's settled. I will call the man "parson." That's how Carl came to address someone of the man's calling. Meanwhile, Chantel was beginning to explain the next step of following available clues.

"So, you see, Carl, you can go with me and we'll check out people that might have known your wife and boys," Chantel announced. "Or we can rely on the proposal of my father. He assures me he knows some of the long-time residents of the community. I am sure he can find some of these people to speak to about your family. Long-time residents would certainly know people who moved here in recent years and recognize those names.

That suggested path of action seemed good to Carl. He could see the value of asking the helpful parson to question some "senior residents". Carl hastily offered pertinent questions to pass along for the parson to ask. "Did you know my wife, Malinda Hatcher and my boys?" "When did you see them last?" "How about their where-abouts after the fire?"

Armed with these and other questions, the parson began his walk around the town, retracing steps he had taken in past weeks. It was a clear, sunny day and the streets ahead of him looked promising. He looked for older residents who lived in the community and might remember the burned-out home. Surely someone could give answer of the house burning and to the family that lived there.

"Greetings, Mrs. Harkin, how are you today?" Parson Cort asked in the friendly tone that was marked by his French accent. He addressed the woman he knew at the local hardware store. Celia and husband Walter Harkin operated the business that was founded just over 40 years ago. A great-uncle, Winston, migrated to America from England. Mrs. Harkin was as much a presence at the store as her husband.

Parson Briant knew her best because she belonged to the ladies' evening Bible class. The women met Saturday afternoons for tea at Aunt Lilly's home. It was an informal gathering the parson did not want to miss. The lively, alert minds of the eight or so women attending—all in their 60s—were a joy to be around. And oh, the tea and delicious crumpets served at the close of the Bible study were yummy indeed.

Today Celia wore a work apron, blue dress and a small cap on her graying hair. She was tall for a woman and this morning stood next to a display barrel filled with the tastiest peaches in town. She turned toward the parson as he initiated the conversation.

"I have a couple of questions I would ask of you. I am searching for details about a missing family for a new friend, Carl Hatcher. Do you recall the name of his wife, Malinda Hatcher and two boys?"

"Oh, parson, now that is exciting. A missing family, did you say? Do you know anything more about them? Did they live around here?" Mrs. Harkin asked.

"No and yes, Madame," the parson continued. "The family in question did indeed live here. I have no other information than that. Their home is the one burned on the corner of Sycamore and Lane Streets. Following the fire, the woman we are searching for, Malinda Hatcher and her boys, disappeared. Do you have any knowledge of them? Of their whereabouts now."

"Why, parson, I seem to recall a young mother who lived there. She and her boys attended the church shortly before you came. But her attendance was irregular. We invited her to the Saturday Bible study, but she explained she was busy with her boys. She was kind of a home body, I assumed. We did not know the husband. Perhaps she left to join him. Maybe he went to war and was killed, do you suppose?"

"I do know the person in question, Carl Hatcher," the parson explained. "I just met him. He is very much alive, I assure you. He is just returned from serving in the army and came home to find his family missing."

Ending their conversation, Parson Cort took polite leave and crossed the street. There he encountered Gladys Rolling, a woman as plump as she was tall. She waddled as she walked, and she talked in similar fashion. Her clothing exhibited garments she could have bought at the latest ladies' goodwill sale.

"Good day, Mrs. Rolling," as he addressed her. "I am on an errand for a new friend, a man who returned from the military and found his family gone. A fire destroyed their home at the corner of Sycamore and Lane Streets. Do you know anything about a Malinda Hatcher and her two sons?"

"Ah yes," responded the rotund Mrs. Rolling. "Ah do, you know'd. I r'member the fire started by an ole' oil can explodin.' The fire spread right jolly and soon the 'ole house was ablaze." This lady seemed to know a bit about the fire's origin, the parson thought.

"Do you know what happened to the occupants of the house?" the parson pursued.

"Ah yes, the poor lady and her two little boys, how sad. They were away visitin' and were spared the terrible fire," she rejoined."

"Wonderful!" excitedly cried the parson. "That means the family is still alive. Wonderful," he exclaimed again as if he had discovered a four leaf clover in a fertile field. "Do you have any other memory of the family? Their whereabouts now?"

"Ah, no, I have no idea," responded Mrs. Rolling, who did indeed provide a major clue in the mystery. She was responsible for affirming the fact of the family's absence at the time of the fire.

And so it went. Parson Briant talked to, respectively, Susie Painkiller, the doctor's wife; Gertie Measure, wife of the town counselor; and Maggie Cash, whose husband was bank president. He was able to confirm that the wife and sons of Carl Hatcher had indeed survived the terrible fire that consumed the family home. Alas, he still did not learn their present whereabouts.

The parson went to locate his daughter and her confidant, the re-tuning soldier who had a great mystery to unravel. Where were they to be found in this fair-sized city? He left them on the street corner next to the bank and went there to begin a new search.

Carl and his new friend, the so-named "sleuth," were even now comfortably settled in a local eatery catching up on information gained thus far. As they spoke, their conversation began to turn toward more personal sharing. They exchanged family values and lessons learned as being part of that experience. And they began to see they had much to appreciate as they talked.

"All right," explained Chantel, "we are here today and dining just like an old couple. And we have learned that the telegram you sent to your former wife in Chicago . . . "

"Chantel, wait a moment," Carl protested. "Malinda is not my former wife. She remains my first and only wife." He was of a mind that she keep that relationship correct. He did not yet realize their past husband-wife arrangement had been rudely annulled by action of Malinda's father. Considering the social standing and marital status of his elder daughter in their new residence of Memphis, Thomas Mason advised Malinda to wipe away all memory of marriage to Carl Hatcher. She was to relate to society that the father of her two sons had deserted the family in an alcoholic stupor. That he was unable to find his way home and, for good measure Thomas surmised, was killed on the road by marauding soldiers looking for deserters. Subject closed.

In that Memphis culture, a thriving riverboat town in1862 when it was captured by Union troops and occupied by lead officer Gen. Ulysses S. Grant, the city was decidedly pro-slavery as past lifestyles were difficult to reform. President Lincoln's 13th Amendment to abolish slavery in the United States was passed by Congress January 31, 1865. But it was only ratified in December after Lincoln's death and Andrew Johnson's presidency began. The amendment prohibited both slavery and involuntary servitude and granted power to Congress to enforce. Tennessee was a typical southern state to realize it must abolish slavery first and only then could it rejoin the union. This it accomplished with minor alterations. It became the first state to rejoin the Union after the war, but slavery remained an issue long after and was practiced by a small group of white citizens.

It was in this fractured setting that Mr. Mason thrust his family. He earnestly believed they could regain their upper-class standing and that his daughters—one now widowed, the other married—would come to occupy "proper" family status. This was important to the Masons as their position in Memphis would allow owning some slaves as before but also endorsing the amendment in question vocally.

Carl naturally could not know of the Mason family's circumstances. Or of the advisement by Malinda's father opposing their marriage ties. Nor could he know that one person in all of Chicago had knowledge of the Hatcher house burning. Homer Justice, now living in that big city, might possess all the clues Carl could hope to obtain. Perhaps Mr. Justice could even have answer as to where the Hatcher family had gone after the fire.

"Let's get this marriage between Malinda and myself correct," Carl continued. "We may have parted on less than amicable terms when I left for military duty. But it is not uncommon for a husband and wife to disagree. We had several disagreements because Malinda was a strong-willed woman with her roots in the South. So, yes, we clashed on that issue constantly. Nonetheless, we had a mutual respect and love for each other."

"Oh goodness, I certainly meant no harm in my comment. It was only to say that your present wife is your former wife because she is not present with you now. Does that make sense?" the now befuddled Chantel tried to sort out. Was her explanation a clue to a building new relationship with this army man? Was she attracted to Carl because he had lost a marriage companion or because she was becoming more and more his only female friend at this time? Was her desire only to help the troubled man or was it a means of building a more intimate friendship? She could only ponder that in her heart. Her emotions were doing strange things to her as she and Carl dined together over muffins and tea in the comfortable atmosphere of the eatery.

"May I pour you more tea?" Carl interrupted her deep thoughts. Here was this handsome man sitting across the dining table from her in present time. Was she sure of her intentions of helping him find himself out of his own lostness, or was it something deeper in her nature of being naturally helpful?

Carl, on his part was wondering just what the woman sitting across the table was thinking. He had gained profound respect for Chantel. Could he share those thoughts of sincere affection with her now at this present time?

"At last I found you two," Parson Briant interrupted their thoughts, joining Carl and Chantel in the small dining room. He breathed a sigh of relief as he seated himself across from Carl. He was tired after managing numerous on-the-street interviews. All morning he had talked earnestly with local citizens to gain knowledge of the young man's family. He had much to say but some questions still to be answered.

"Allow me to tell you that I have found some of the answers you consigned me to as I visited with some of the nice residents in town," the parson reported. He proceeded to state that his respondents had told him they knew of Malinda and the two sons. He said he learned the Hatcher family had escaped the fire and that they were likely all in good health. As to their whereabouts, the parson explained he had no information.

Carl accepted this information with seriousness. He had to admit that with the parson's summation of the interviews he had to conclude his family was hopelessly vanished. He gave voice to his present situation, explaining that he had arrived at a decisive point in his life.

"I have come to this conclusion," Carl began to slowly explain to the parson and to his daughter seated at his left. "I have decided to close the door to my past and live in the present. To do this," Carl considered carefully, "I must have faith to face the future, because that is where my life must proceed.

"I plan to sell my swine business and invest the income into purchasing the local saw mill and lumber yard, as I learned it is for sale. I can thus engage my engineering skills learned in the army. Doing so will continue to remind me of the present day and not belabor the past. I will start building my own new house first and then see what is next in my future path.

There is one Bible passage, the only one I am afraid, that I learned in life. It goes something like this, "Trust in the Lord with all your heart; do not trust your own understanding. In all your ways look to God and he will manage your paths" (Carl's translation, Proverbs 3:5-6).

If I can follow this teaching, surely the enterprising citizens of DeKalb will need construction and new home building as the city grows. There, I've said it. I want to make a fresh start and feel deserving the opportunity after what I have gone through. I feel better for making these decisions," Carl concluded.

Parson Briant and daughter Chantel both breathed out exchanges of awe at their friend's startlingly new choices. He was willing to leave his past at the back door and make plans to walk through a promising front door. His future was before him, and Carl expressed himself as ready to pursue that future regardless of what he had to leave behind.

"What a statement of looking at possible ways to direct your future," Parson Briant imputed. As he made this declaration, the parson noticed the bond, the growing attraction between his daughter and this young man. He saw that Carl was finally returning home from military service and leaving the awful Civil War behind. He wondered how far this relationship between Chantel and Carl Hatcher would grow.

"Wow, what a future you must have in mind!" exclaimed Chantel. She especially wanted to share with Carl as he worked to develop his new plans. Did she have a place in his present life and his forward-looking future? Almost to answer her silent thoughts, Carl continued to speak.

"You, parson and especially you, Chantel, have supported me in this current search of locating my missing family. Thank you so much. I look forward to knowing you both better. Perhaps, I can inquire of the time for Sunday worship and seek out a renewed church path. Your daughter, parson, has convinced me your name, as I understand from Chantel, means 'bold or wise counselor.' I sincerely hope I can rely on your knowledge and helpful guidance in following my new path.

"And, Chantel, I understand your name means 'place of stone' or 'song,' and you have certainly been strong as stone and made music to me. I would invite you to help with clues to building my new home, if you are into that type of detective work. We have partnered well in these past events, and I hope we can continue our relationship into the future. Your present assistance could lead us into a dynamic future."

"Oh, Carl. You don't know what that means to me," Chantel said happily. She, at 27 was old enough to know she was of age to be married. She could hope this handsome military veteran would come to feel the same way as they traveled together. Case closed.

THE END

Carl and new friend Chantel face promising new future together.

Epilogue
Carl and Chantel Share Romantic Feelings

After Carl gives up hope of finding his wife Malinda and two sons, he courts Chantel to complete the cycle and set the record straight. His DeKalb city record affirms that he was a Civil War veteran and a farmer. It was to the farming occupation that he returned with an optimistic look toward new adventures ahead, possibly with such a pleasant companion as the charming Chantel Briant. Carl envisioned his farming business and the lumber mill operation he had recently purchased would use his background skills well. Still, he had a nagging feeling that would not go away about the family he left behind.

Review Questions for
Hatcher Family Myth: Deserter or Hero?

CHICAGO IN CIVIL WAR DAYS
1. What reasons did Carl have for traveling to the "windy city" by train?
2. Was Carl practical about his reasons for going to Chicago?
3. Is Chicago a city you would like to visit? Why?
4. What is important about Chicago's 1860s steel production? Can you give details?
5. Did Chicago provide significant materials for Civil War use?
6. Who benefited most from Chicago's production industries, North or South?

CARL MEETS SOUTHERN BELLE AT THEATRE
1. Why was Carl bored with the Livestock Convention after several workshops?
2. Why was it important that his friend's ticket became available to Carl?
3. How did Carl meet Malinda Lee at the theatre? Was she impressed?
4. What did Carl learn about the 19-year-old Malinda immediately?
5. Who were Malinda's companions at the theatre? Why was this important?
6. Was Malinda completely honest about taking the theatre seat offered by Carl?

CARL AND MALINDA DESCRIBED
1. Who made the first decision in Carl and Malinda's relationship? Why was this important?

2. Do you think the new couple saw each other as portrayed in the photograph?

3. How did Carl's losses of younger sister and parents affect his approach to life?

4. What encouragement did his uncle Raymond and Cecilia Hatcher give to Carl?

5. Were Carl's actions in introducing Malinda to his pig farm and piglets accurate?

6. How did Carl react to the home Malinda's parents lived in? How did Thomas and Deedee see Carl at that first meeting?

CARL ASKS FOR MALINDA'S HAND

1. How did Carl and Malinda's affection grow in a such a brief time? Was this normal?

2. Did Carl present a suitable case to Thomas Mason for gaining Malinda's hand?

3. Why was Malinda's wedding and presentation into society arranged together? Did the older Thomas Mason have hidden motives for this debutante-presentation / wedding?

4. Describe Carl and Malinda's feelings about initial days on the farm?

5. Did Malinda have good reason to want her second child born at a Chicago hospital?

6. What made Malinda's role as mother a challenging one? How did her mother assist her?

CARL CHOOSES FEDERAL CAUSE OVER MALINDA

1. What contributed to Carl's decision for joining the Union Army?

2. How did Malinda respond to Carl's insistence to support President Lincoln?

3. What in their cultures contributed to Carl and Malinda's views on North and South?

4. What view was Carl expressing by stating he firmly opposed a system that bound one person to work for another, denying individual freedom, regardless of color?

5. What did Malinda mean by stating, "Having slaves is an important part of culture in the South!"

6. Why did the Mason family own slaves who did service for them in assigned ways?

MALINDA DECRIES HUSBAND'S ABSENCE

1. How did Malinda's reaction to her husband's absence affect their sons, John and Willis?

2. What did the sons miss most about their father's absence?

3. Was Carl's' humor with the boys helpful when compared to Malinda's stricter nature?

4. What was older John's example and influence on younger brother Willie?

5. Why did Carl take a second job outside of farm work? Was this beneficial to him for the future he chose?

6. How did Malinda react to Carl's second job and arriving home so late?

CARL ENLISTS IN 1LLINOIS UNION ENGINEERS

1. What was the detailed description of Carl's army uniform? Why was this important?

2. Why was Carl promoted to an assignment normally occupied by West Point graduates?

3. What contribution did the Corps of Engineers make to the war?

4. Why did his supervisors find such favor with Army Pvt. Carl Hatcher?

5. What was Carl's part in Gen. Sherman's decisive march through the parched South?

6. How did Carl's farm background contribute to his heroic action in saving two of his men in the unfortunate explosion? Why was it important that he was awarded the Union Army recognition of Valor?

CORPORAL HATCHER CONTINUES BUILDING ASSIGNMENT

1. Why did Col. Randall assign Carl to help in rebuilding the depleted southern states?
2. How did Carl react to his new assignment? Was he satisfied with his new command?
3. Why did Carl feel his connection with Sherman's decisive march could affect relationships he might have with southern landowners?
4. What did Col. Randall do to relieve Carl's fears in taking the new assignment?

HATCHER JOINS THE RECONSTRUCTION

1. Was Corporal Hatcher content to remain in his Union Army assignment in the South?
2. Why was the South's Reconstruction seen as a complex undertaking?
3. Why did learning history of the southern states become important to Carl?
4. What did Ms. Famer (affectionately known as "salt and pepper") bring to reconstruction efforts through contacts with southern businessmen?
5. Why did Mr. McGinty's actions oppose President Lincoln's Thirteenth Amendment?
6. During this time, how did Carl try to maintain contact with his family in Illinois?

MALINDA FOSTERS OWN MISERY

1. Was Malinda's behavior a suitable response to her husband's absence?

2. What role did Jurgens Hench play in overhearing Malinda's expressed discomfort?

3. How did Mr. Mason's comments further Hench's dislike of southern complaints?

4. How did Neil, Stout, and Henry Limber identify with Jurgen Hench's judgments?

5. How can Jurgens be identified as a "mob leader," one who calls for group action to something they saw as wrong?

6. What does the group decide to do to "teach Malinda a lesson" she won't forget?

FIERY ATTACK ON THE HATCHER HOUSE

1. What is a "vigilante crowd"? How can their action lead to social disruption?

2. What caused the intense fire that destroyed the complete Hatcher residence?

3. What good fortune saved Malinda and the boys from the burning home?

4. Why did Homer Justice inform Mr. Mason in Chicago about the fire that destroyed the Hatcher home but want to remain anonymous?

5. Why did Thomas and Dedee Mason resettle their family in Memphis, Tennessee? Was Mr. Mason wise in advising Malinda to say her alcoholic husband had deserted her?

6. Why is Malinda's response important to Carl's story of "deserter or hero"?

CIVILIAN CARL TRAVELS MISSISSIPPI RIVER

1. How did civilian Carl Hatcher feel about his family upon his army discharge?

2. Why did Carl choose a steamboat to transport him from New Orleans?

3. How do you think Carl felt conversing with a black American who fought on the opposite side of the Civil War? Do you think he regretted not knowing more about Confederates?

4. How important was it that Carl learned about efforts of Harriet Tubman's use of the "underground railroad" to rescue former slaves to freedom in free states and Canada?

5. Why was Harriet Tubman's experience as "conductor of the Underground Railroad" important to Civil War history? Can you name other black leaders of that time?

6. Did Carl's continued concern about his home family show how much he missed them?

CONTINUING JOURNEY HOME TO ILLINOIS

1. What purpose did the Union Army have in "mustering out" Corporal Hatcher in New Orleans, Louisiana so far from his home in Illinois?

2. Why did Carl and his big white stallion King have such respect for each other?

3. How did Carl's work under the authorative Floyd Bickel show his ability to succeed under any condition?

4. Why did conversation with Dino Donatello add to Carl's understanding of the Civil War? Why was it called a war that "pitted brother against brother and even father against son"?

5. What caused the war to bring strangers together and for Union soldiers to help Confederate wounded and vice versa?

HOMEWARD BOUND BUT WHERE IS HOME?

1. Why was riding a passenger train from St. Louis to Chicago possible in the North?

2. Why was Carl's reaction so emotional when he surveyed the burned-out home in DeKalb and realized the worst about his lost

family? Hadn't he seen worse in the evil war?

3. How did the assassination of President Lincoln by an insignificant actor, John Wilkes Booth, affect Carl? Was the response justified?

4. What kind of relief did the sympathetic offer of help from Chantel Briant, the daughter of a new pastor to DeKalb, give the grief-stricken Carl?

5. Why was the return of Carl's telegram to the Mason Home in Chicago just another blow to his hopes of locating Malinda and his young sons?

6. Why did Carl see the often-distracted Chantel as a complete mystery?

MISSING FAMILY'S FRIENDS QUESTIONED

1. When Carl was introduced to Parson Cort Briant, why did he appear uncomfortable in the presence of a man of the cloth?

2. Was the parson's proposal to interview citizens of DeKalb agreeable with his daughter Chantel as well as to Carl? What contribution did Carl make to support the plan?

3. Were Parson Briant's interview efforts successful? Why or why not?

4. Why did the army veteran and the 27-year-old Chantel seem to have a spark between them as they enjoyed each other's conversation?

5. What does Carl's sudden insistence that Malinda should still be considered as his legal wife tell you about his loyalty to his family?

6. What evidence does the reader learn that Carl is pursuing a new direction in his life? Is this surprising for someone who has lost wife and family?

EPILOGUE

1. It would seem Carl has much to consider, facing a past of military experience and now suffering more loss of family members. How does this background challenge his resolve?

2. Do you see a promising future for army veteran Carl and new friend Chantel Briant?

3. Why is it that Carl has a persistent, nagging feeling about the family left behind?

4. Does Homer Justice, the silent participant in the burning of the Hatcher family home, have voice in the future?

5. Will the residents of DeKalb accept Carl Hatcher as the person he is and cordially welcome him home?

6. Will the community recognize Carl and Chantel as a couple who have formed an allegiance that shows their desire to start a new journey together?